FOLIO
Animals and Birds

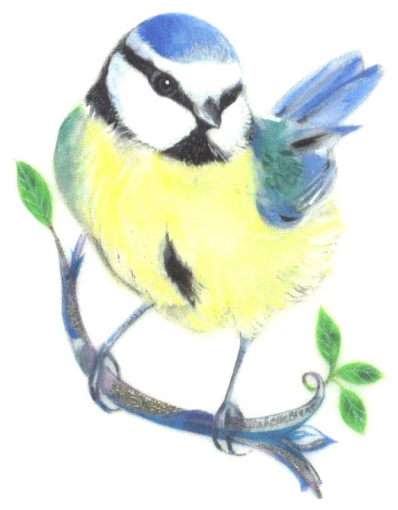

Illuminated by ISABELLE BRENT

www.isabellebrent.com

Copyright© Isabelle Brent
Designed and Illustrated by Isabelle Brent
ISBN-13 : 978-1974245642
ISBN-10 : 1974245640
All rights reserved Isabelle Brent 2017

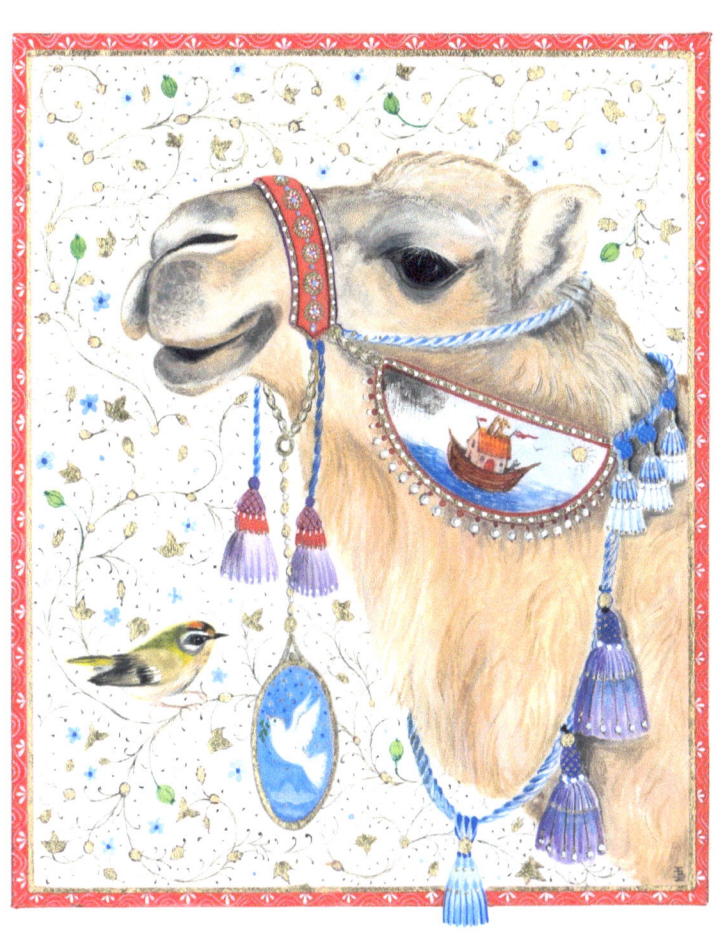

INTRODUCTION

Isabelle Brent was born in England and very early on showed an artistic talent. Between the years of 1984, when she exhibited at the Royal Academy of Arts in London, and 2000 she securely established herself as a successful international illustrator. During this period she illustrated the great classics, Grimm, Andersen, Kipling and Oscar Wilde, many of her titles being translated into foreign editions. In 2007 she settled in France.

In this book Isabelle Brent shows us a world of beauty. The content is never ugly; her subjects are painted in a jewel-like manner. It is not only technique that is presented but also composition, drawing, and observation, combining to make each illuminated picture a work of art. Her works have been compared, by certified experts in historical and contemporary art in Paris, to those of the master illuminators of the Middle Ages.

Take pleasure in the following pages; a small selection of her prolific output and enjoy the richness of her unique illustrations. Each one is painted with watercolour on calf-skin vellum and gilded with hand applied gold leaf.

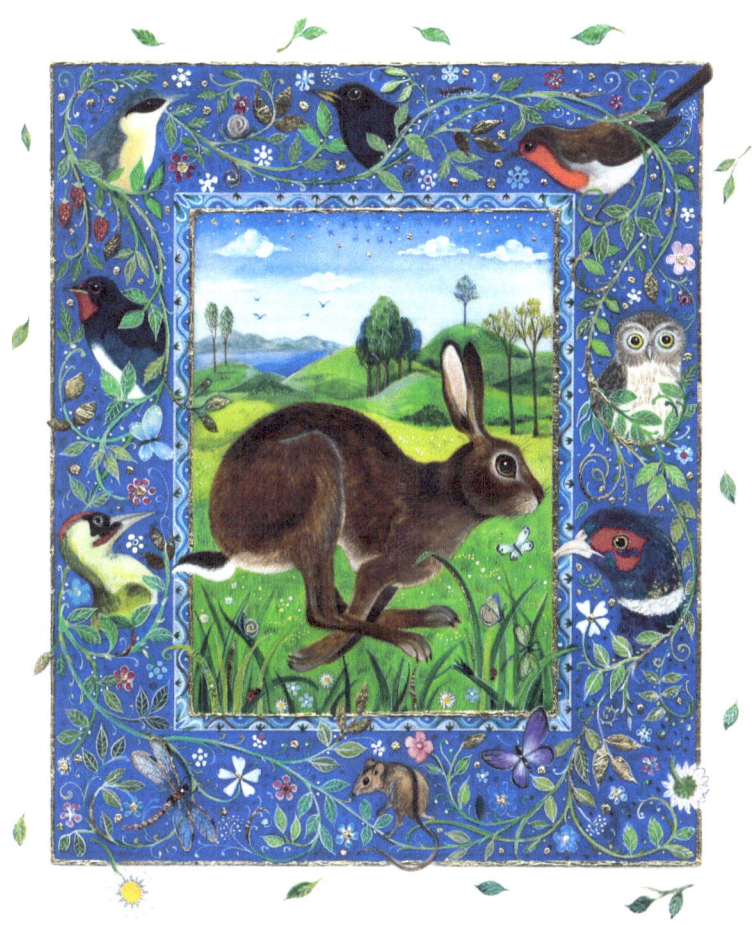

IMAGINE

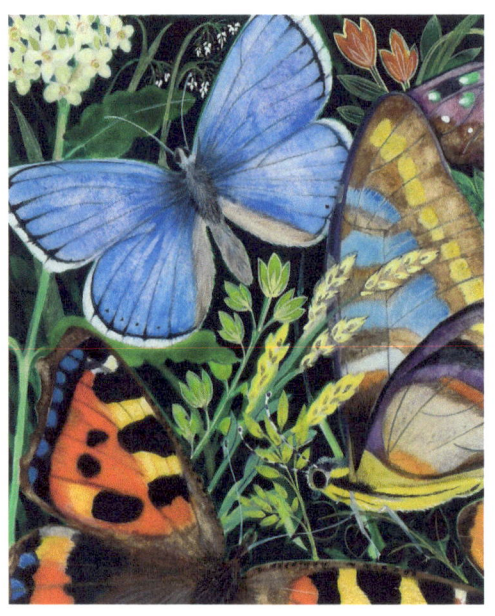

Papillons Symphonie
115mm x 135mm

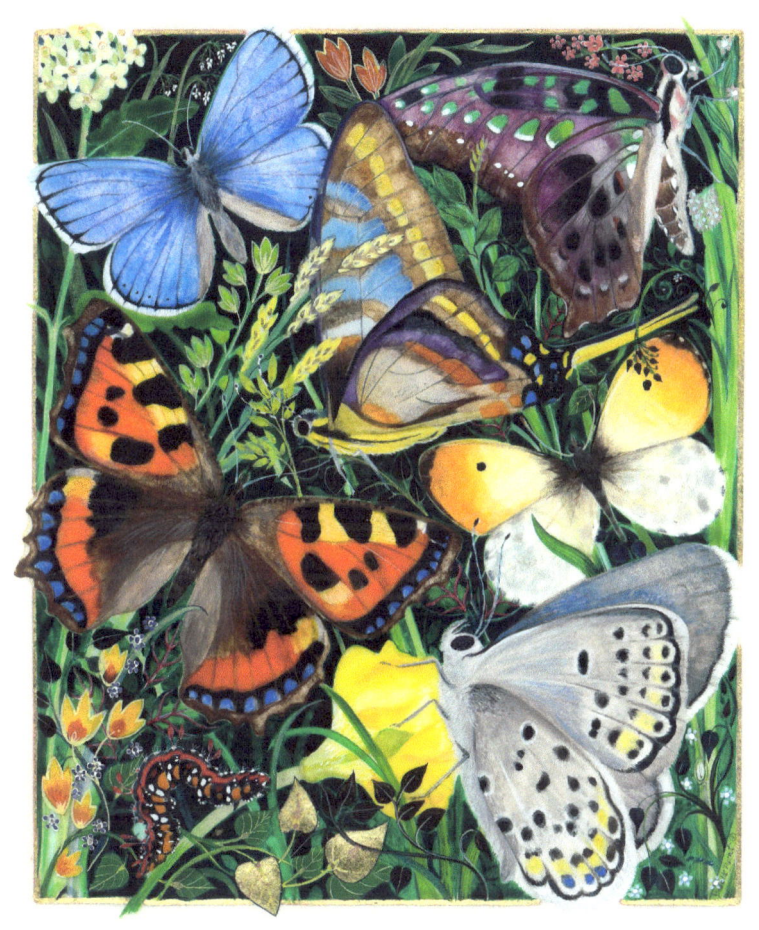

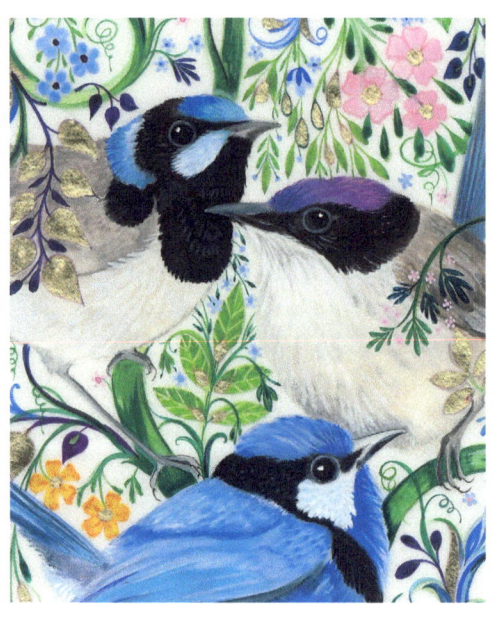

Trois Mérions Superbes
115mm x 135mm

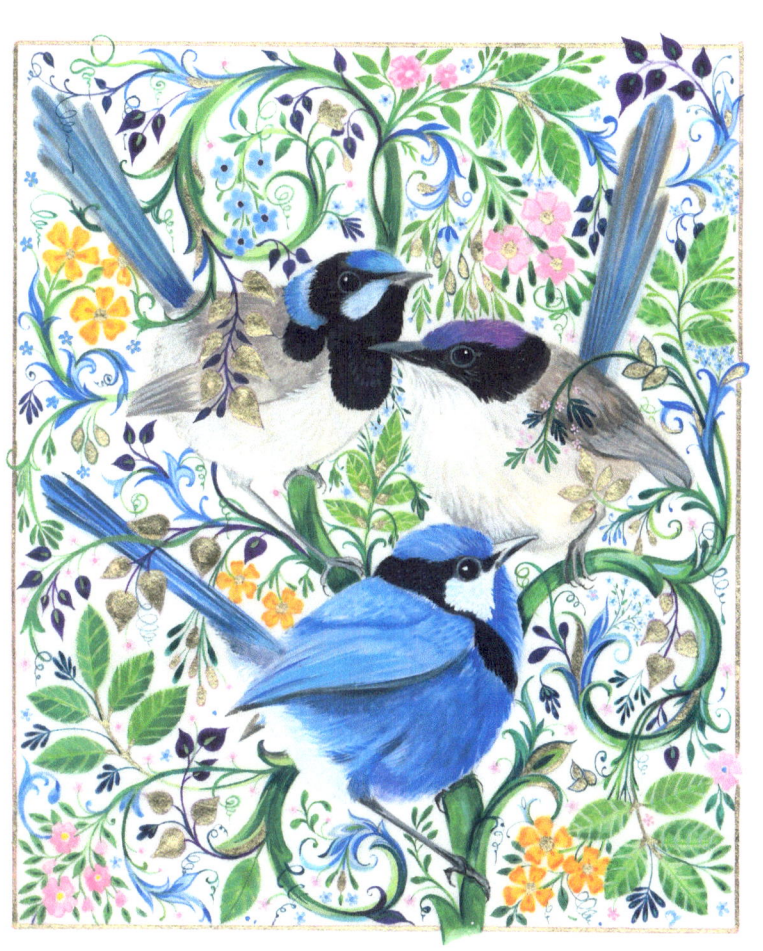

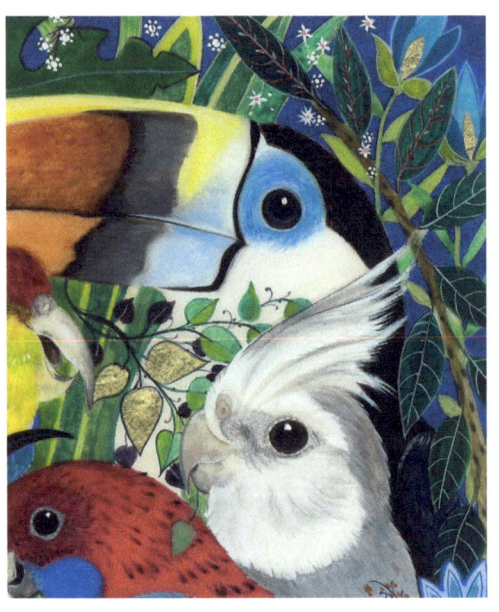

Paradis d'Oiseaux
115mm x 135mm

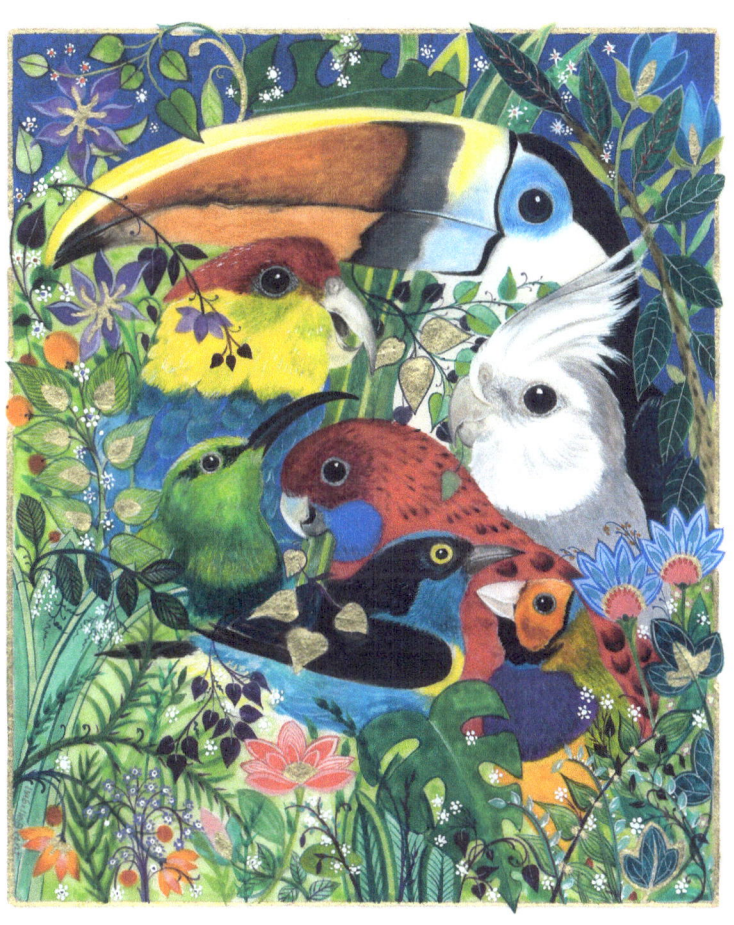

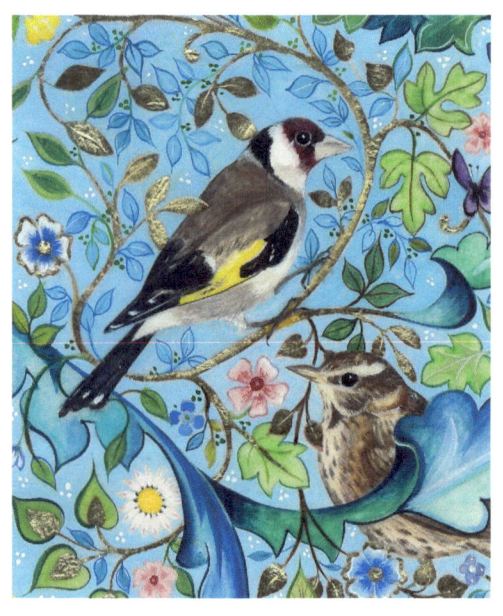

Le Printemps des Oiseaux
115mm x 135mm

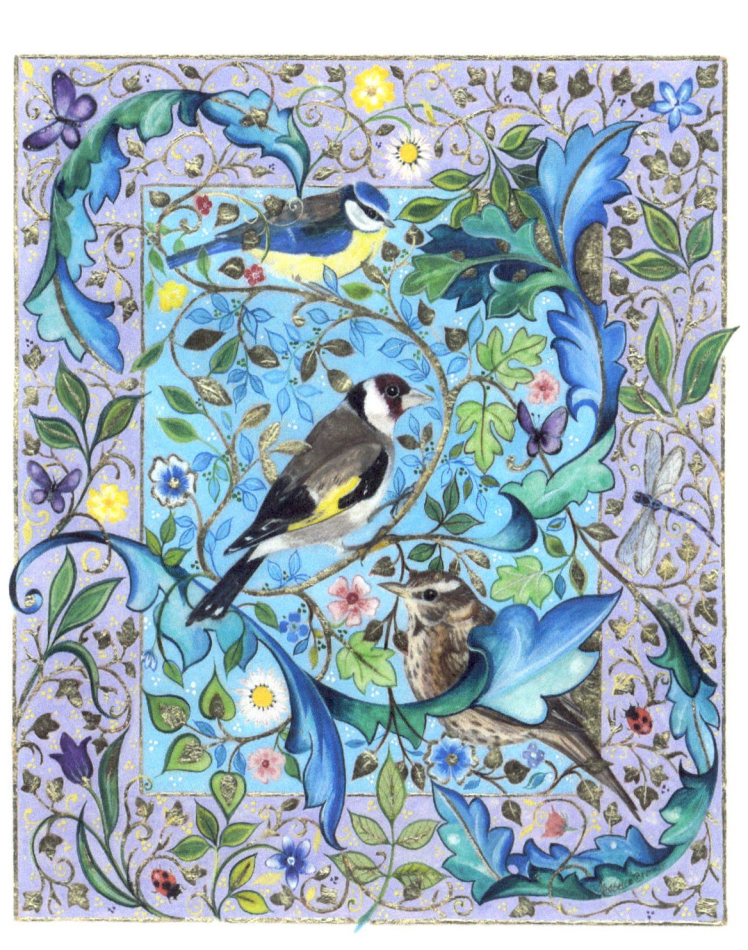

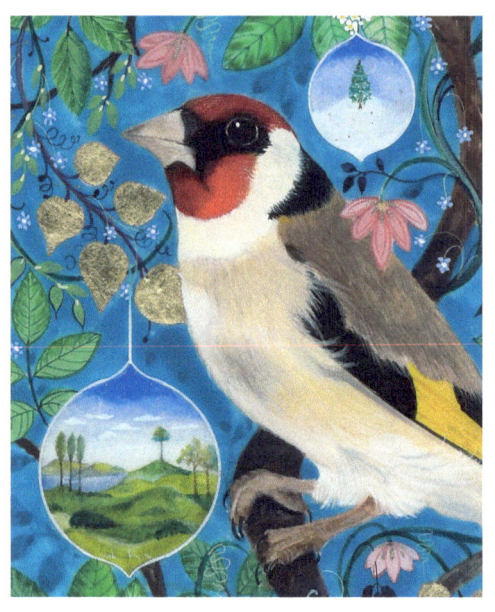

Rêve de Chardonneret
115mm x 135mm

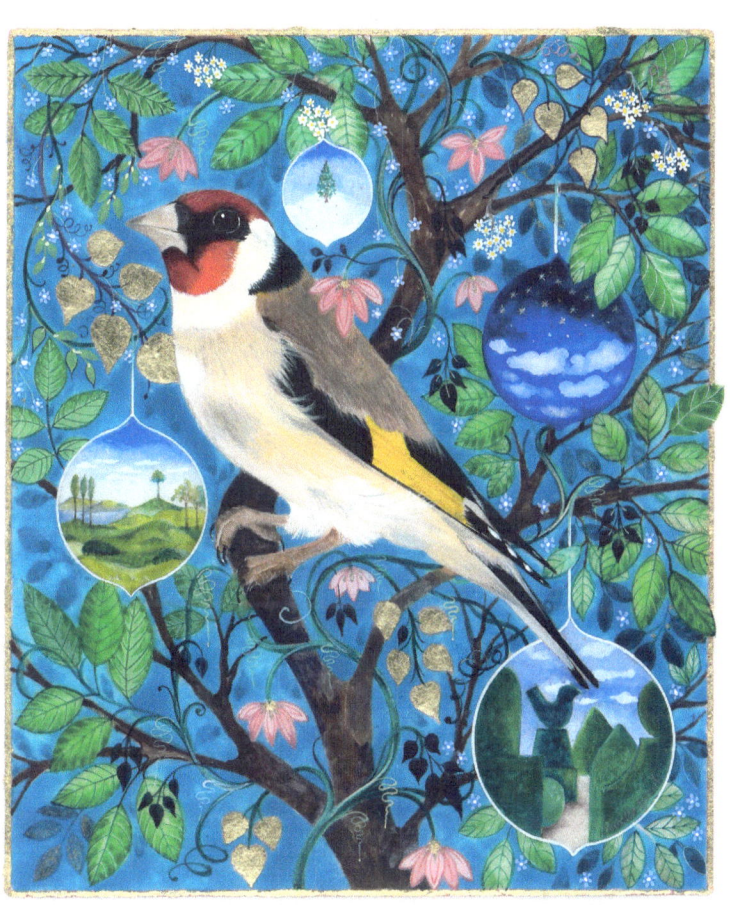

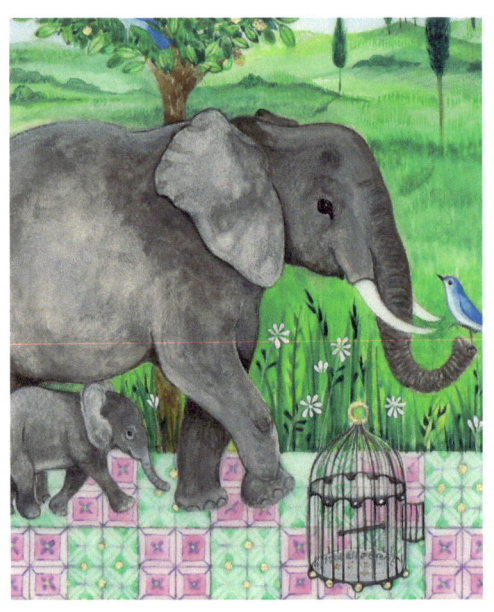

Eléphatissimo
115mm x 135mm

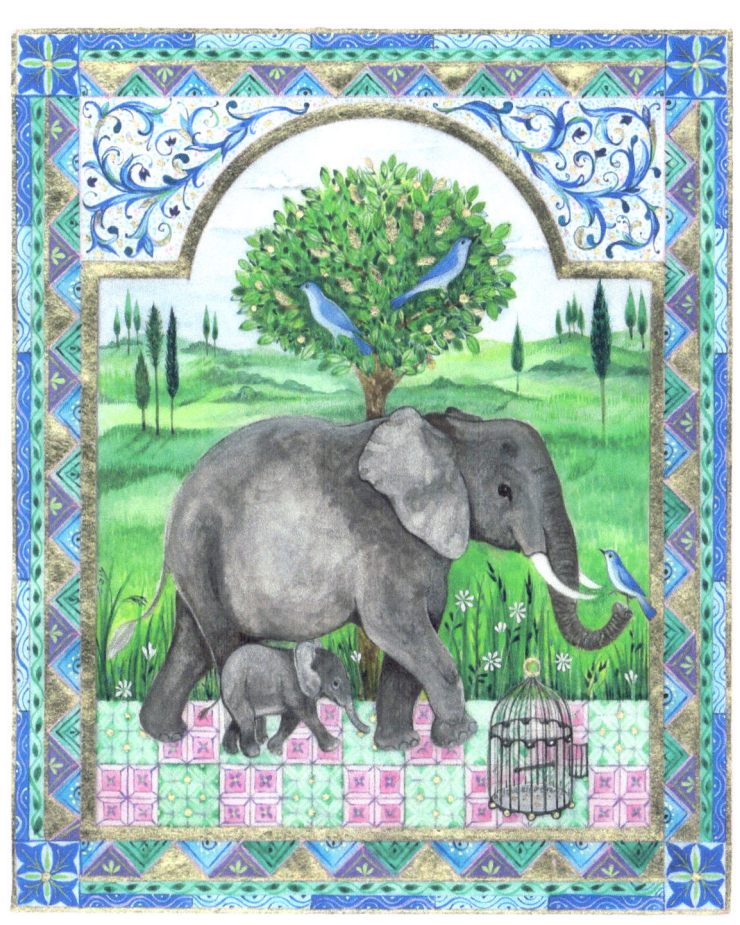

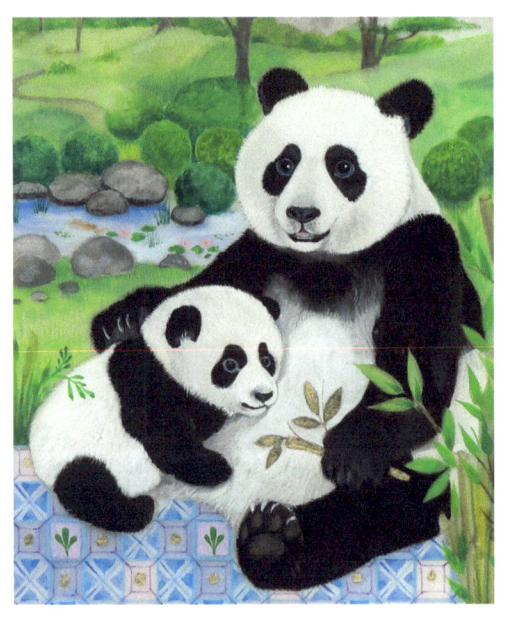

Pandamania
115mm x 135mm

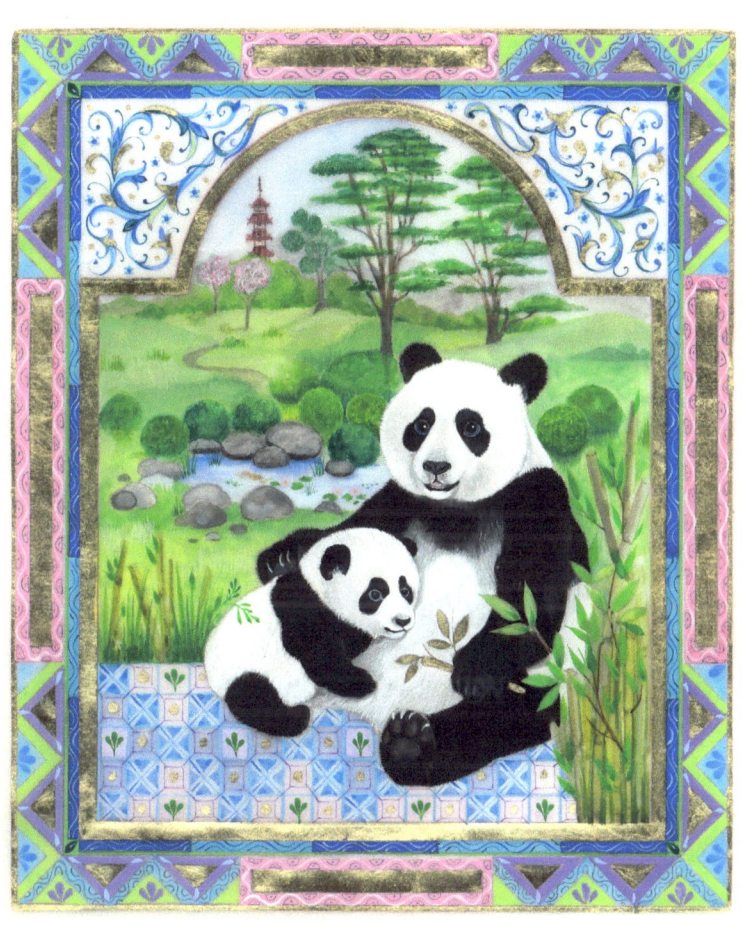

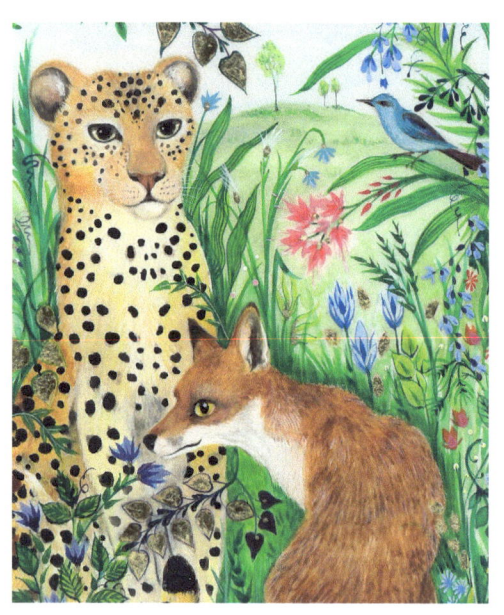

Le Léopard et le Renard
(Fables d'Esope)
115mm x 135mm

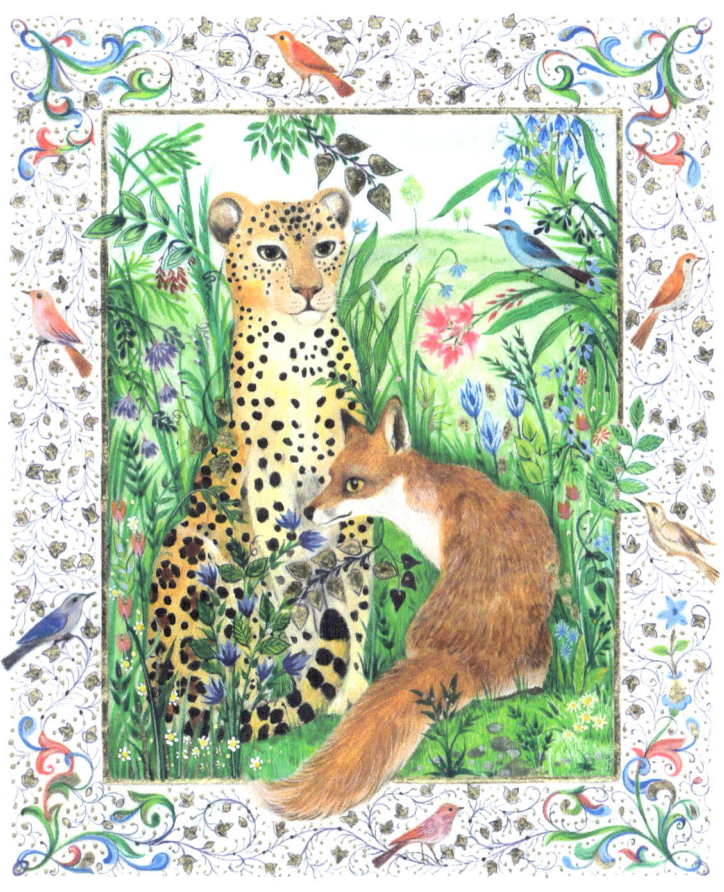

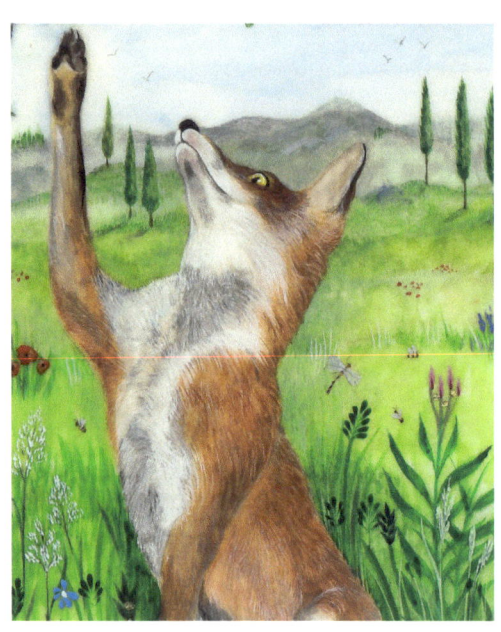

Le Renard et les Raisins
(Fables d'Esope)
115mm x 135mm

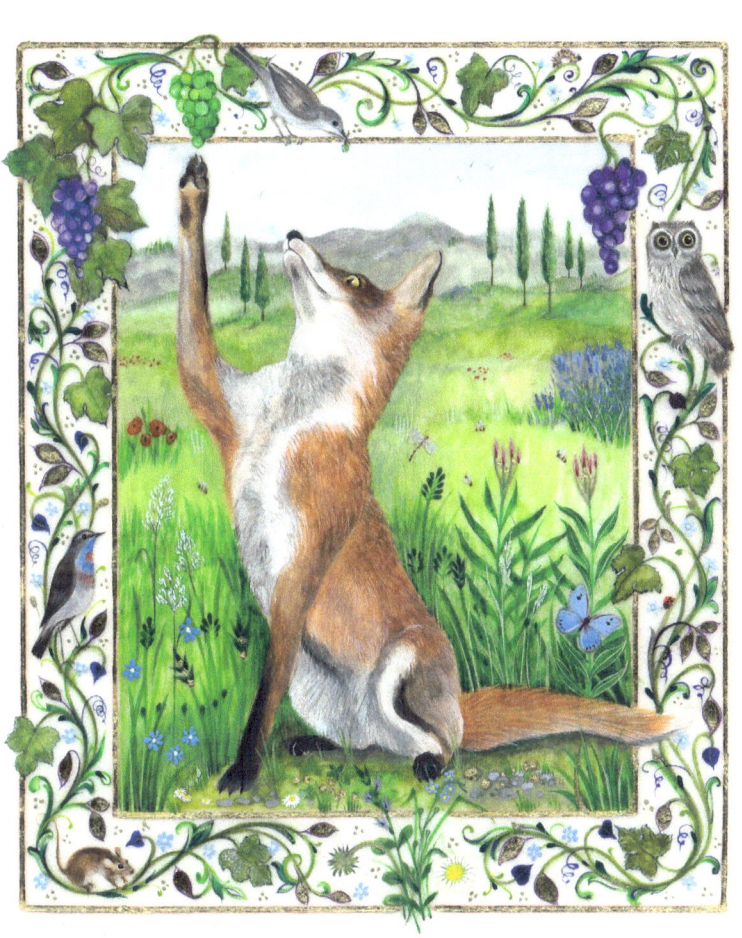

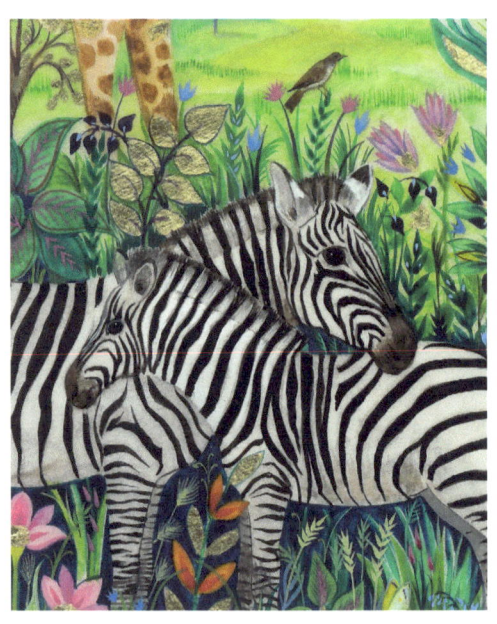

Savannah
115mm x 135mm

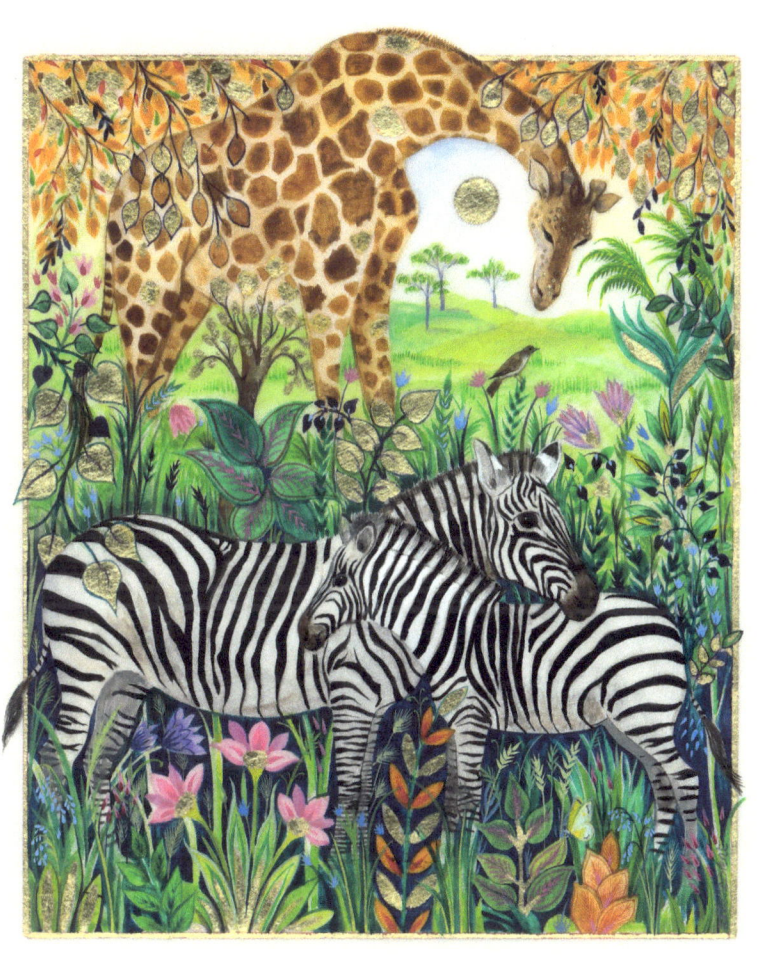

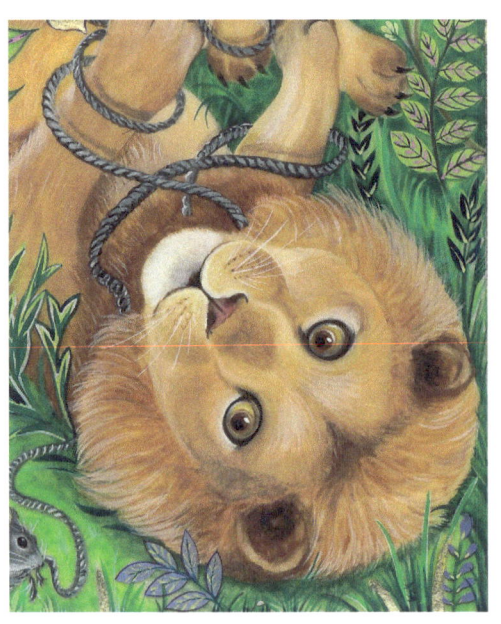

Le Lion et la Souris
(Fables d'Esope)
115mm x 135mm

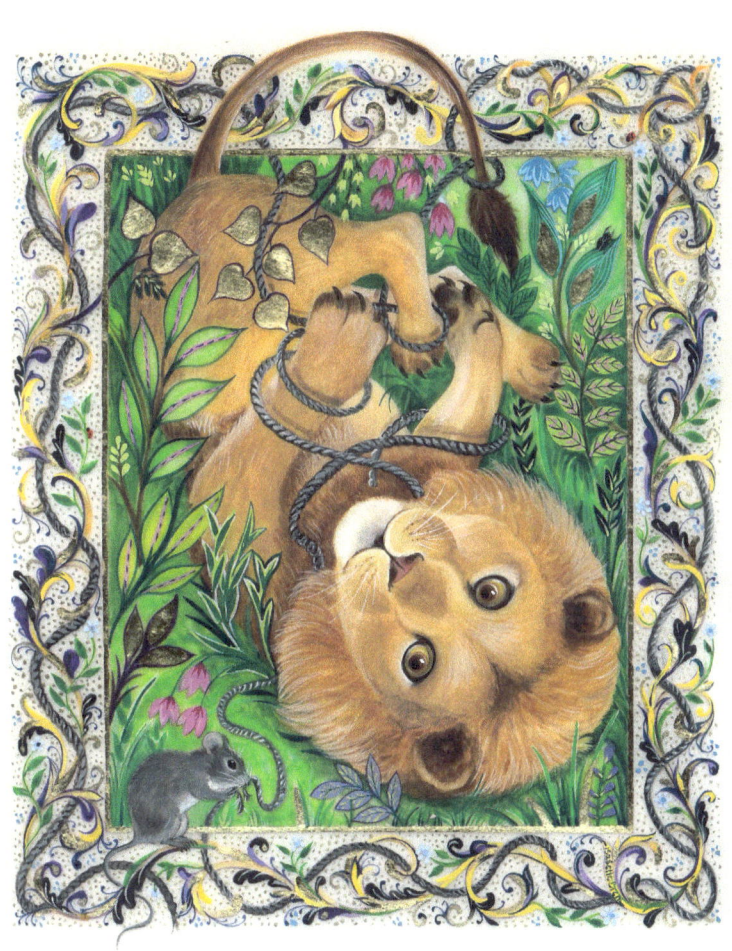

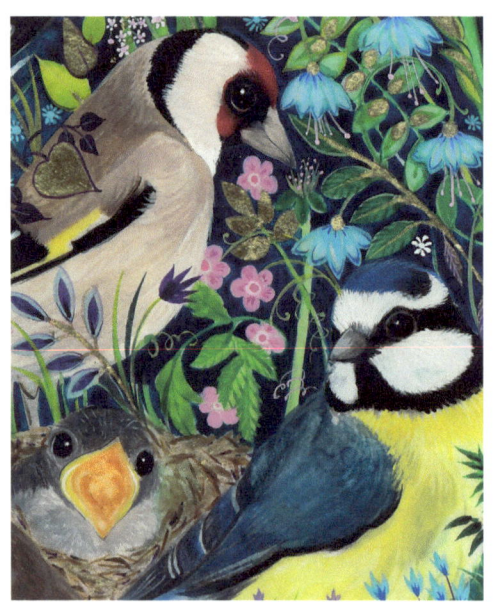

Histoire d'Oisillon
115mm x 135mm

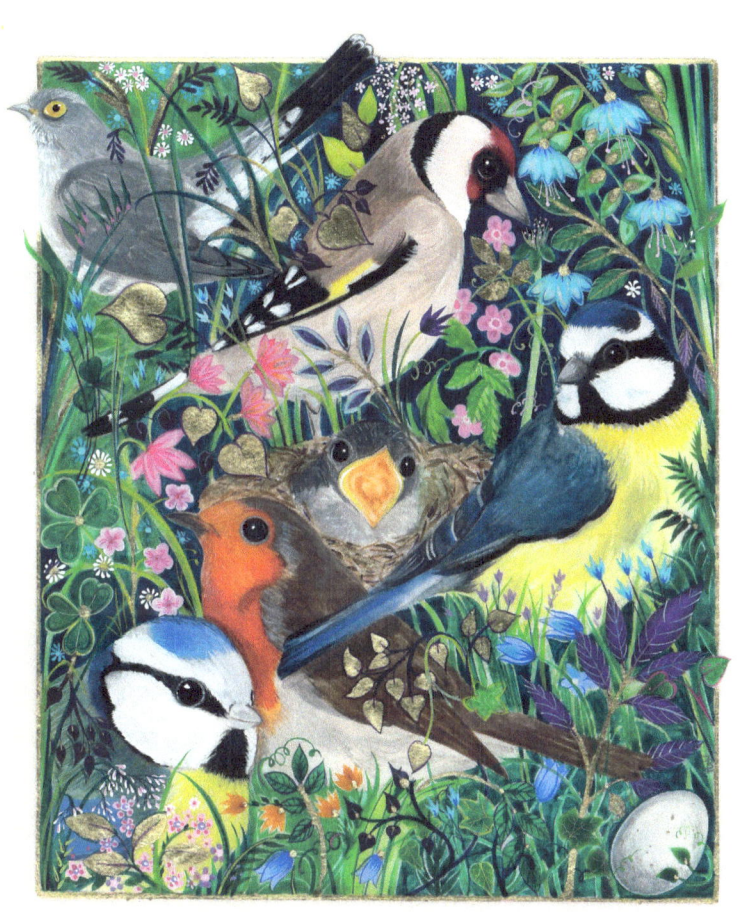

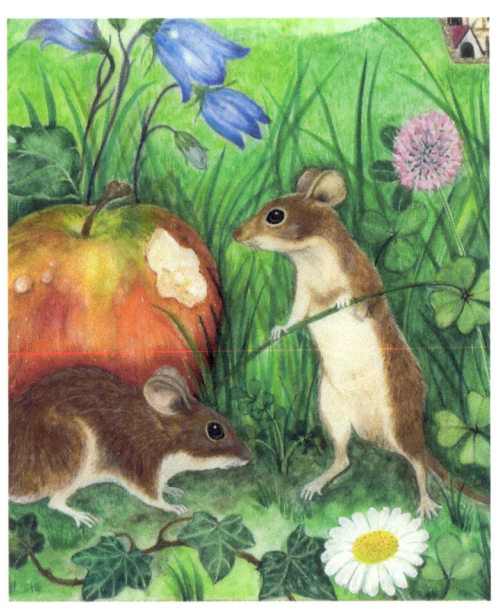

Souris des Villes, Souris des Champs
(Fables d'Esope)
115mm x 135mm

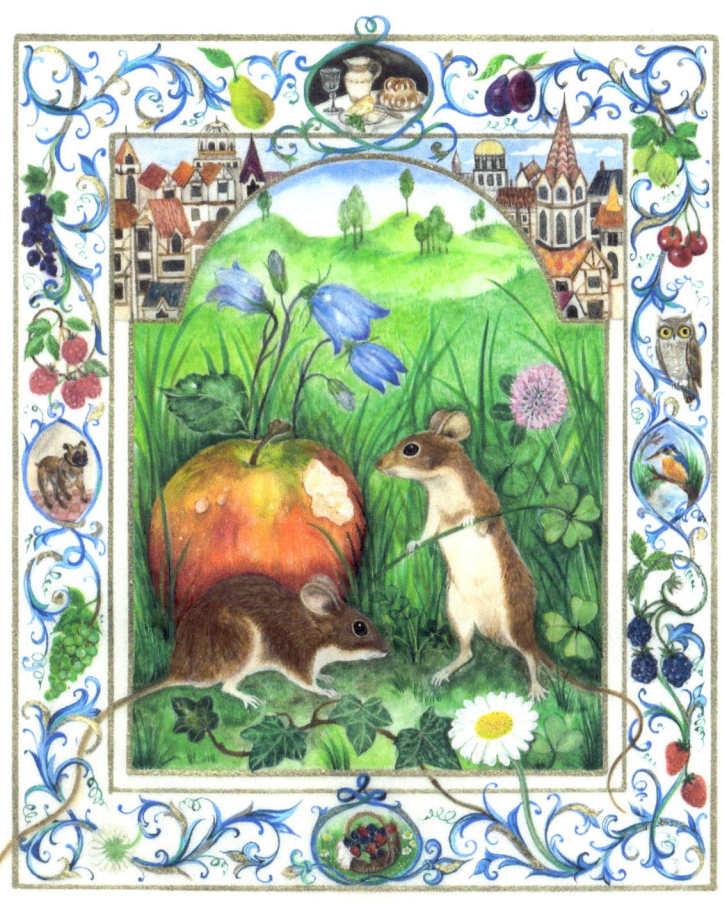

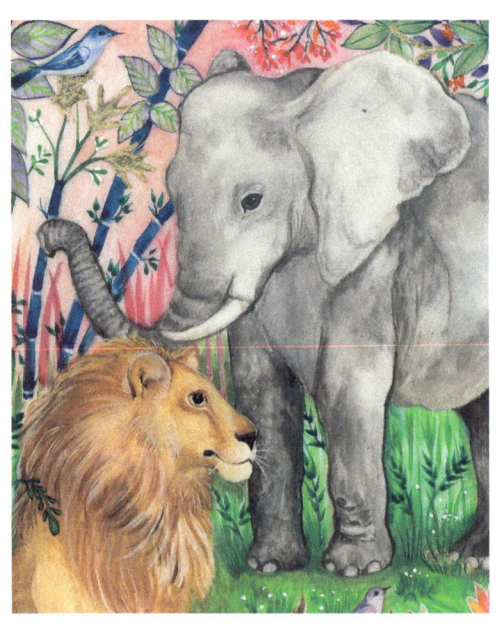

Le Lion, Jupiter et l'Eléphant
(Fables d'Esope)
115mm x 135mm

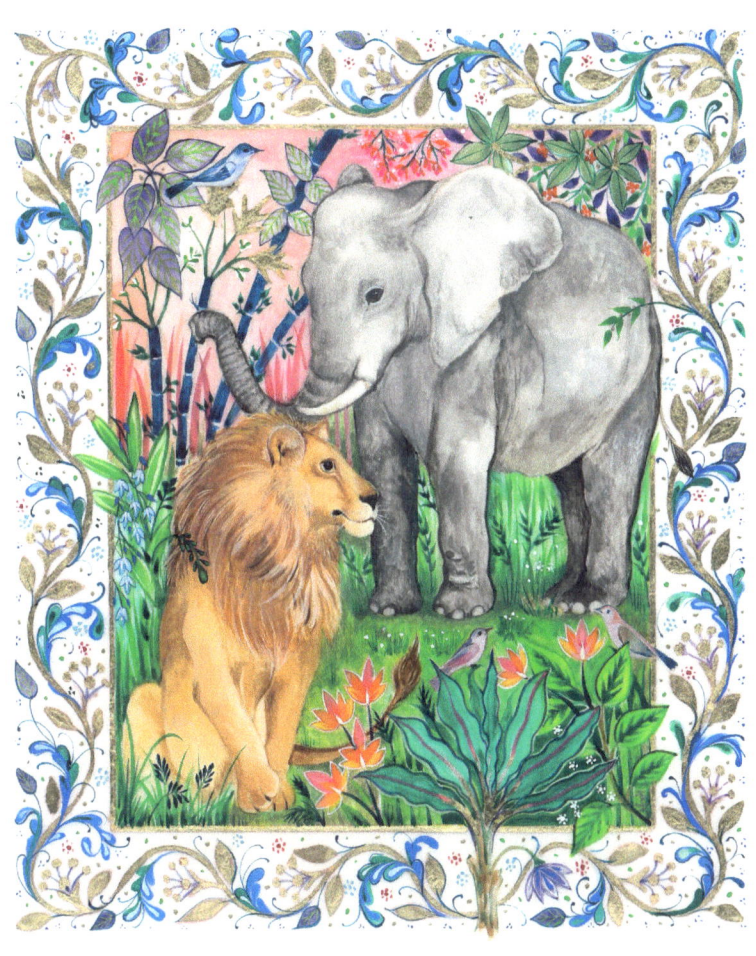

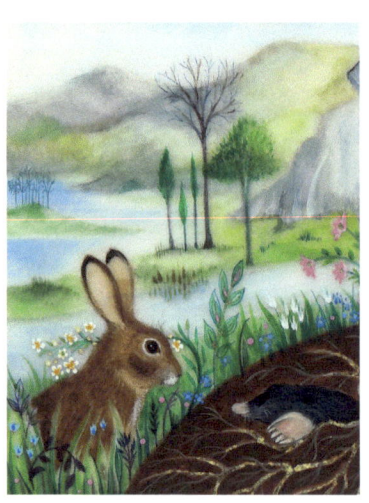

L'Arbre de Vie
115mm x 135mm

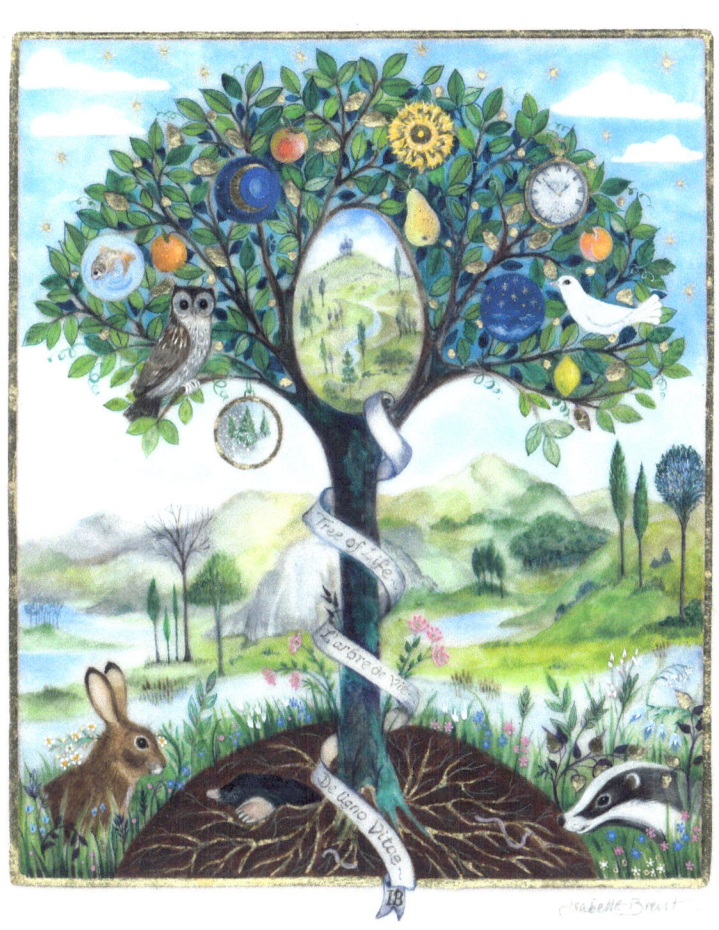

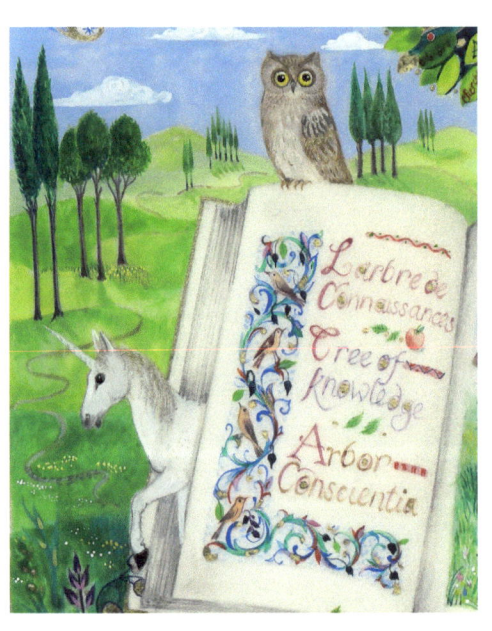

L'Arbre de Connaissances
115mm x 135mm

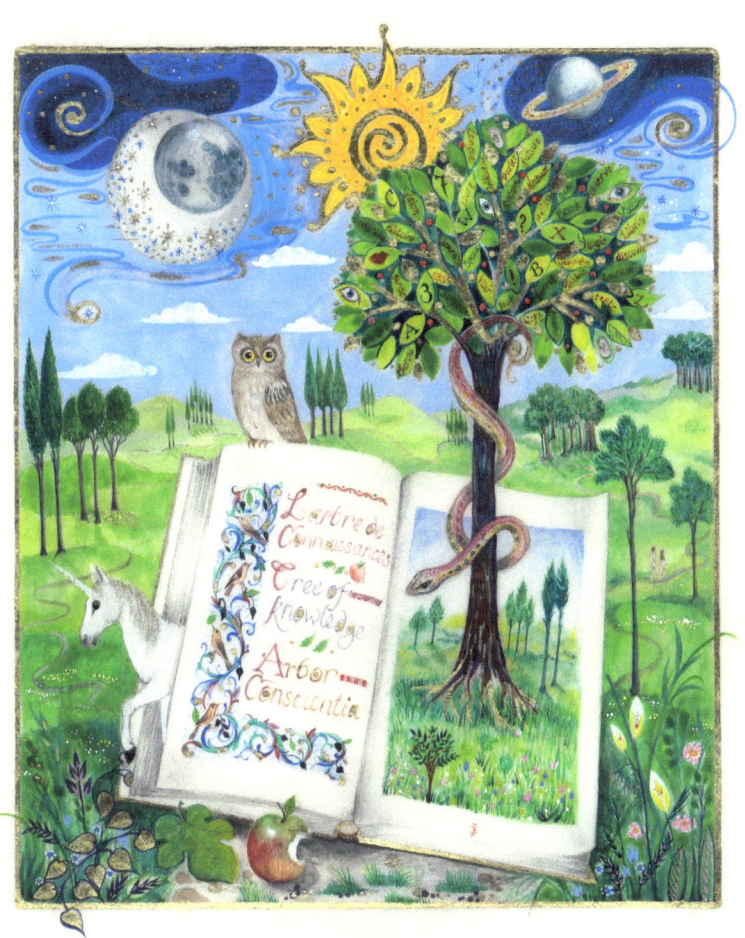

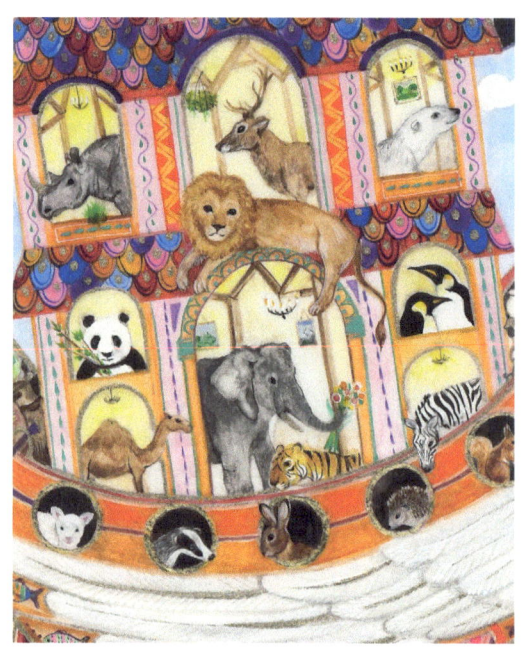

L'Arche d'Isabelle
115mm x 135mm

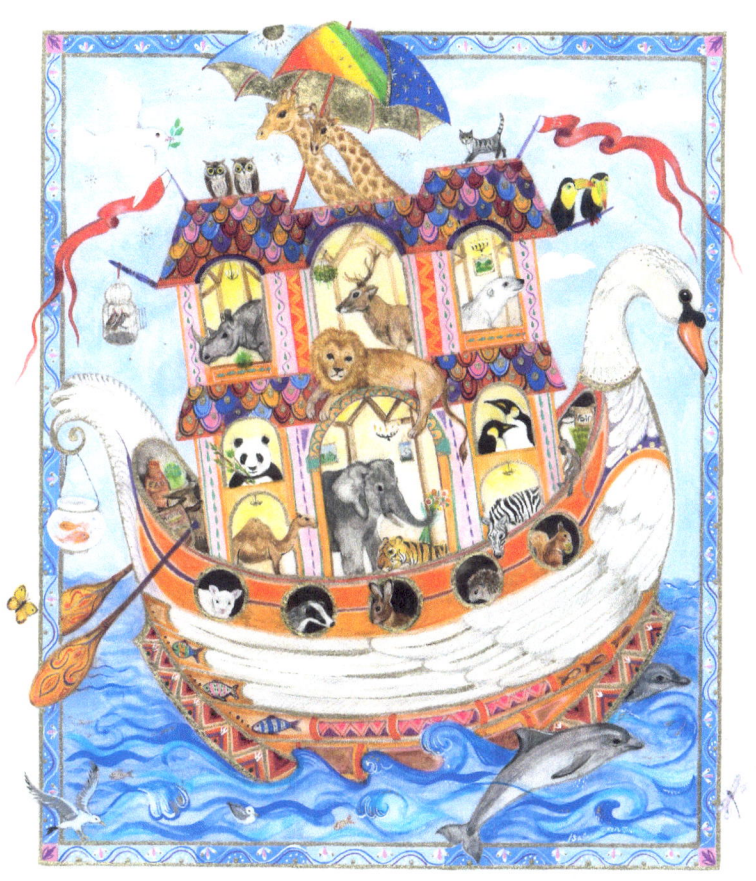

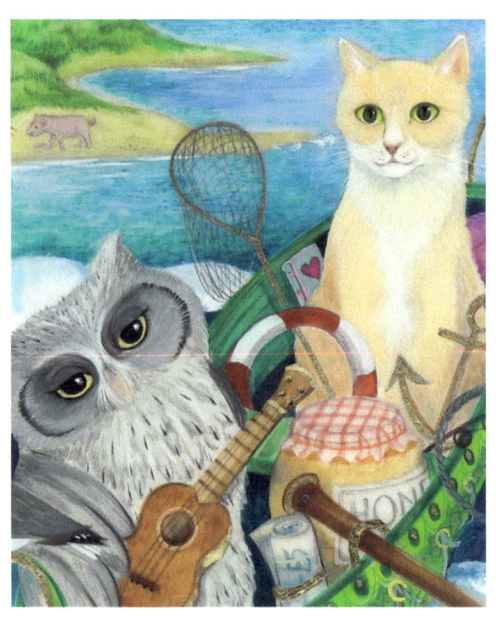

The Owl and the Pussycat
115mm x 135mm

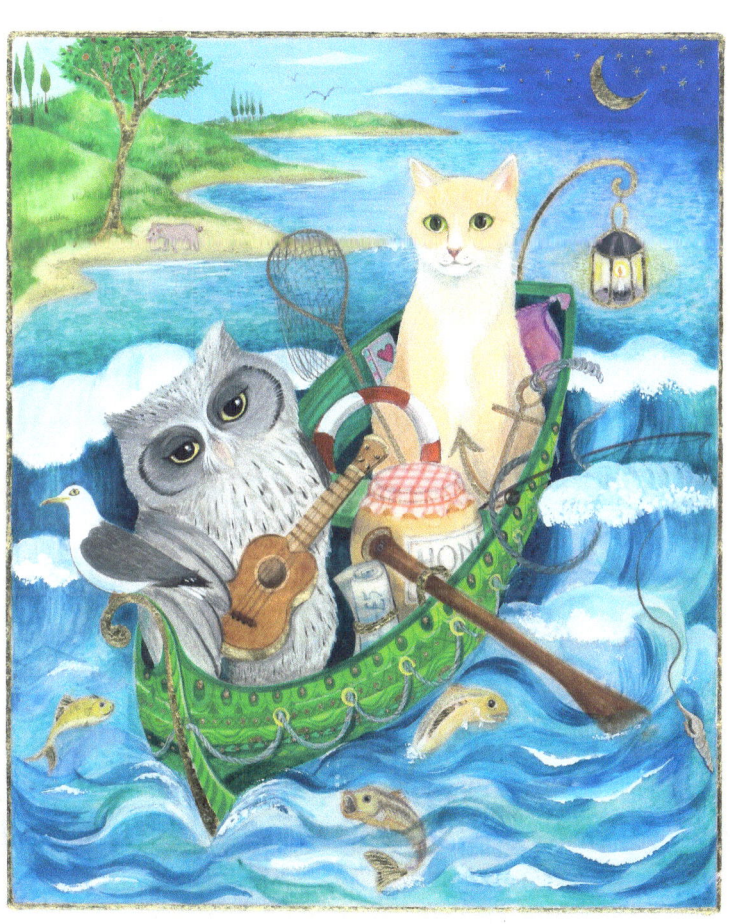

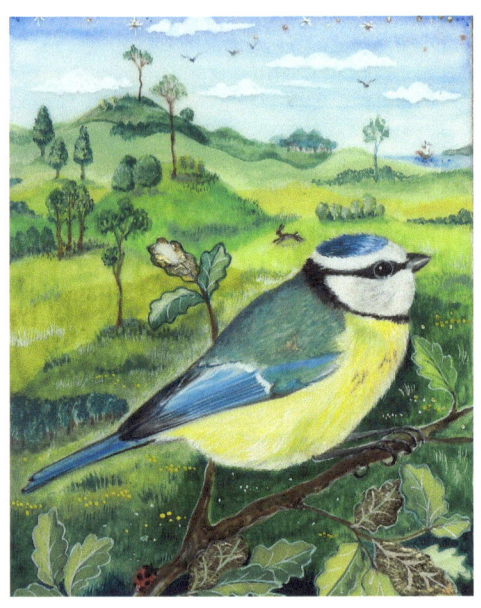

Le Mésange Bleue
115mm x 135mm

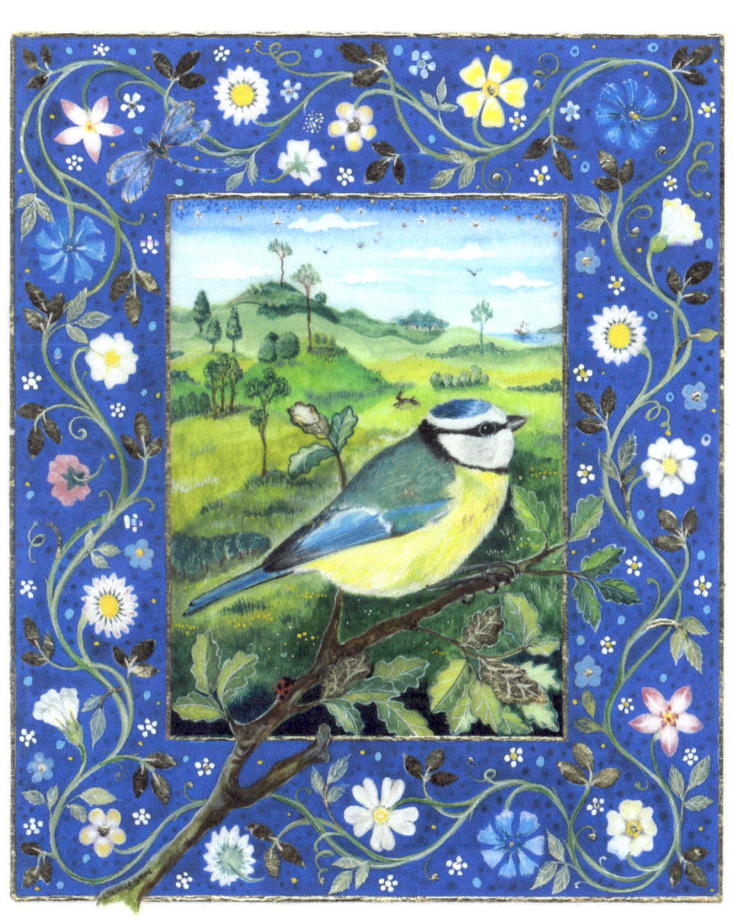

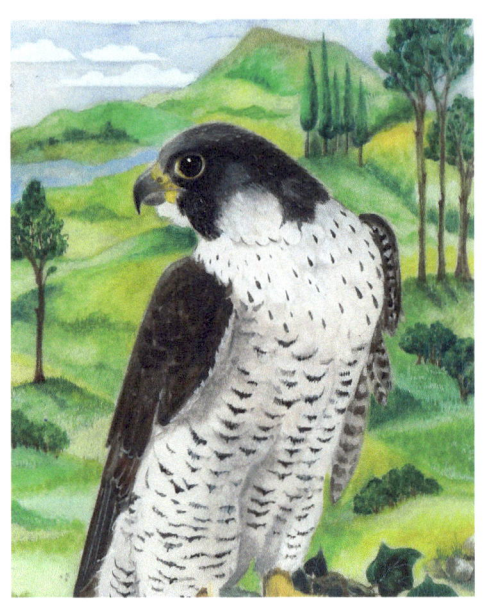

Vie de Rapaces
115mm x 135mm

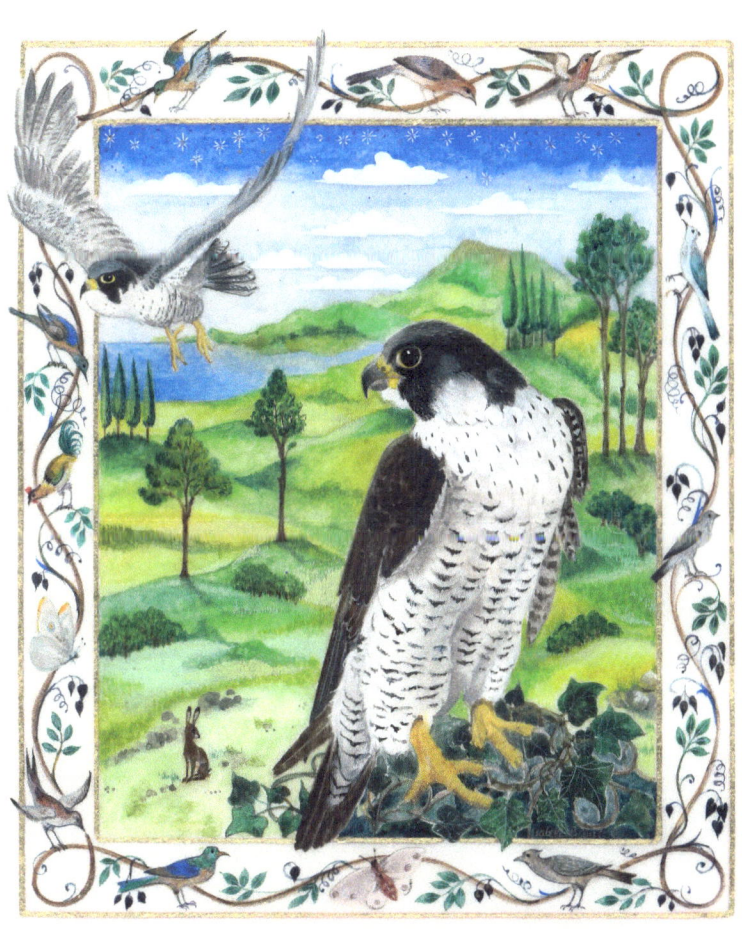

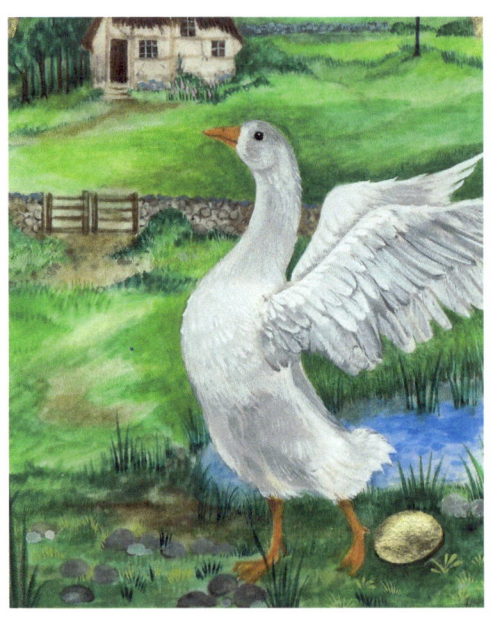

Oie aux Œufs d'Or
(Fables d'Esope)
115mm x 135mm

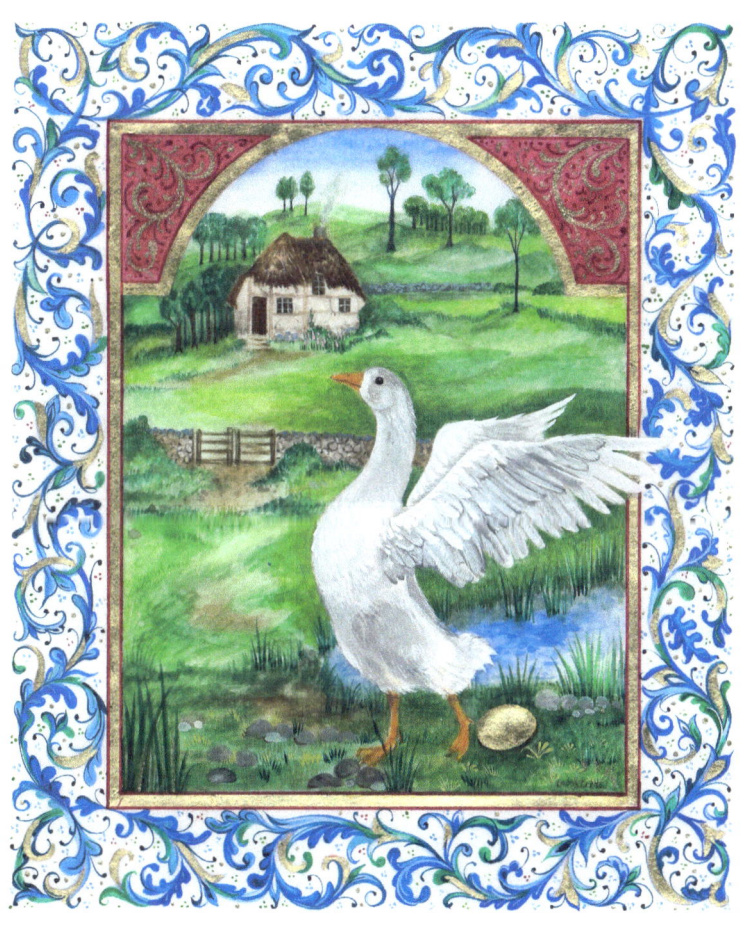

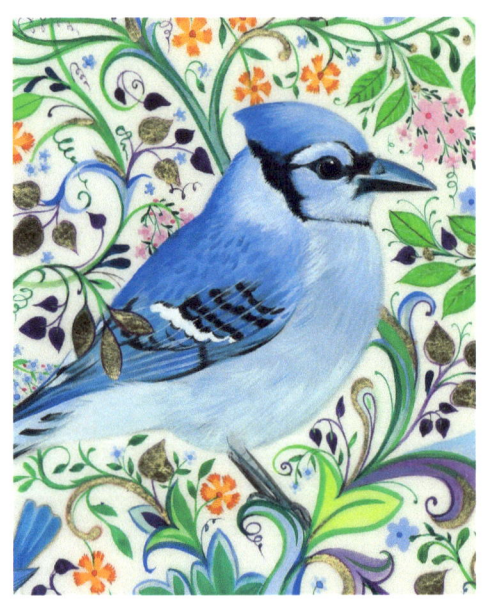

Geai Bleu d'Amérique
115mm x 135mm

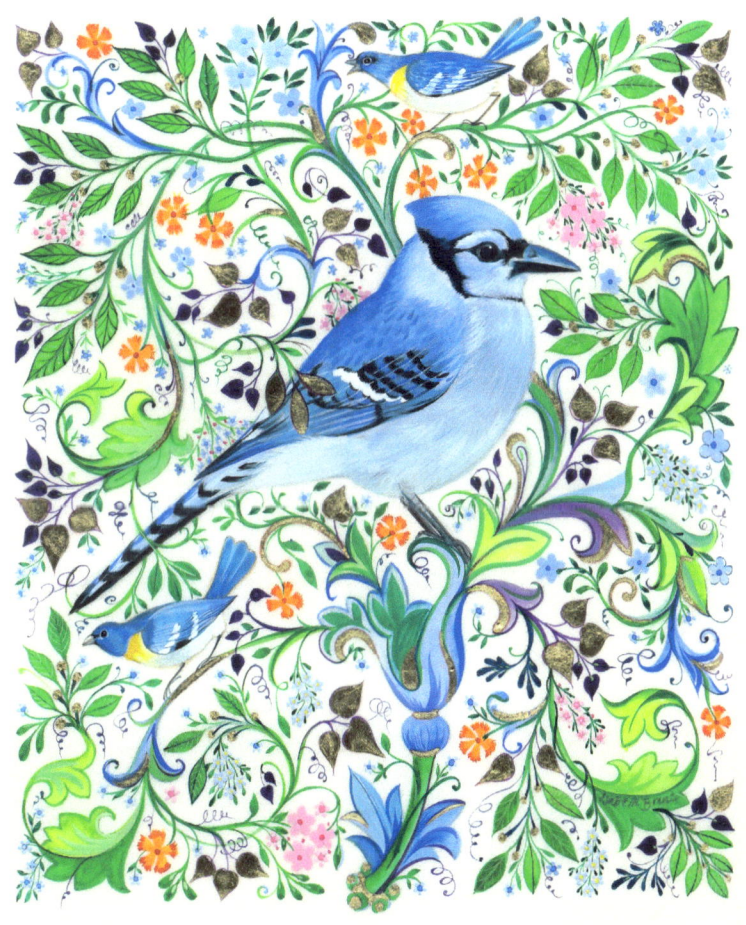

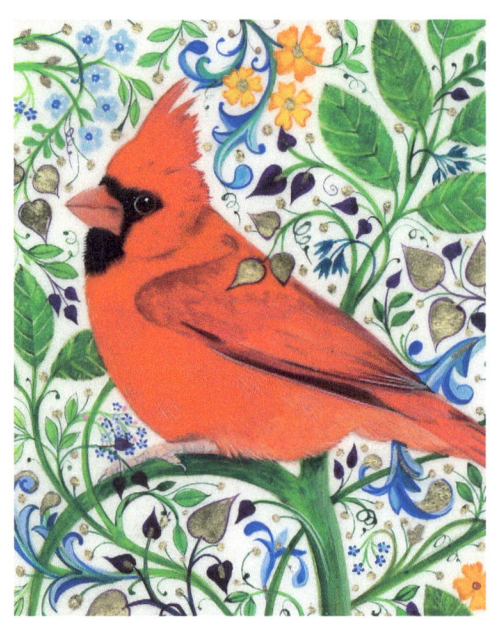

Le Cardinal
115mm x 135mm

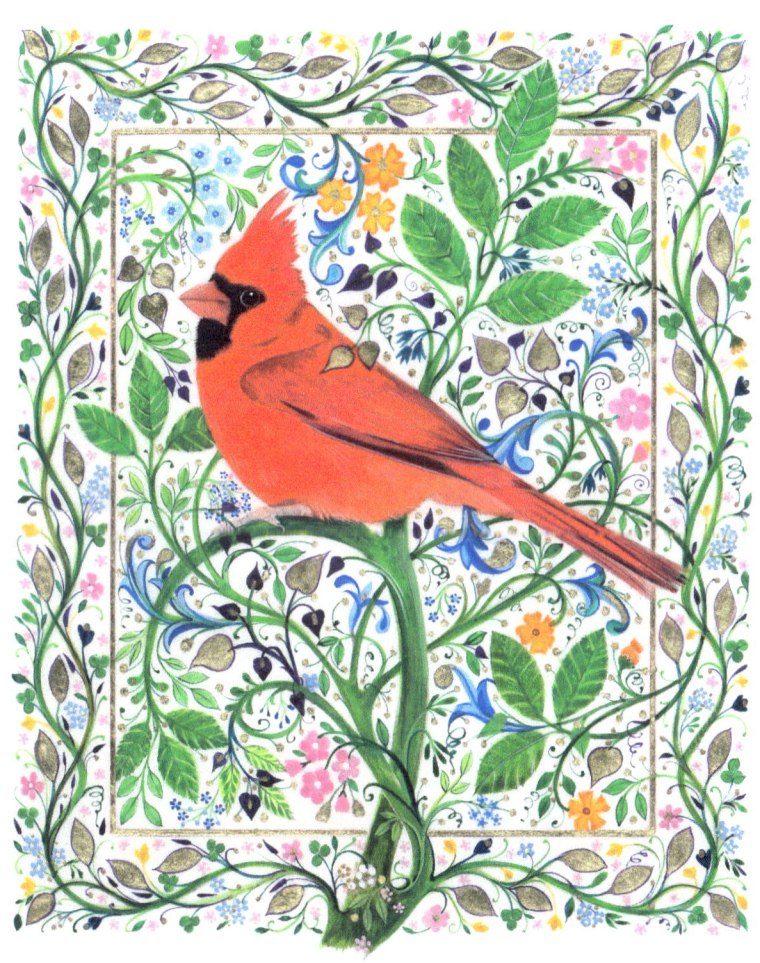

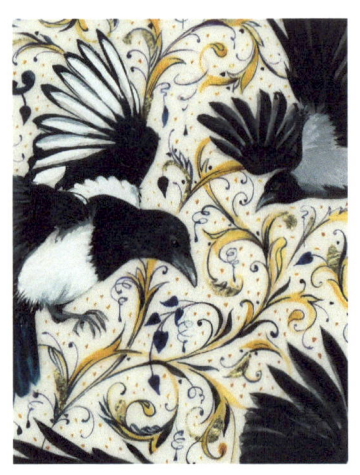

Corbeaux et Pie
85mm x 105mm

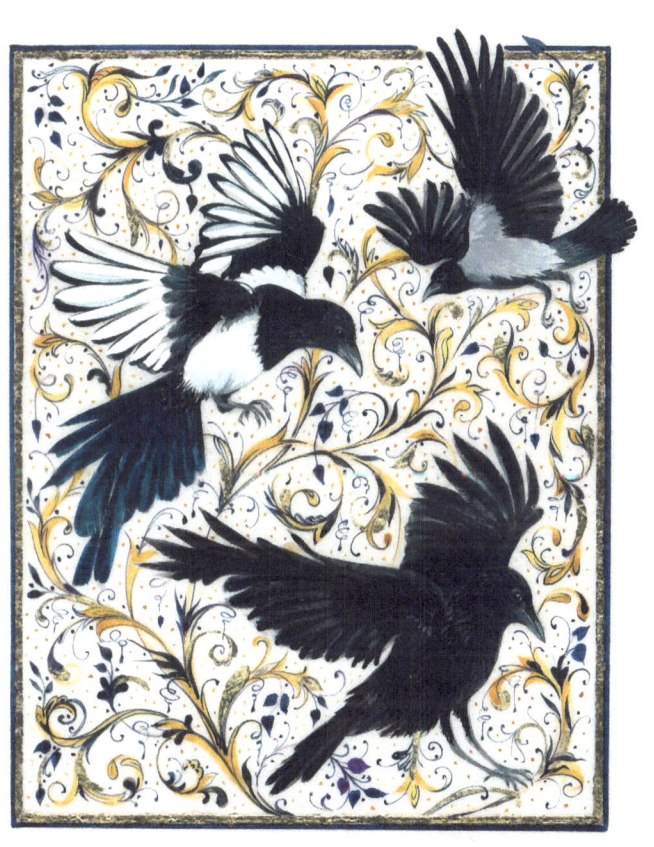

www.ingramcontent.com/pod-product-compliance
Lightning Source LLC
Chambersburg PA
CBHW040242220526
45473CB00001B/344